*

POEMS

*

*

POEMS BY

AUSTIN CLARKE

TONY CONNOR

and

CHARLES TOMLINSON

*

London

OXFORD UNIVERSITY PRESS

NEW YORK TORONTO

1964

Oxford University Press, Amen House, London E.C.4

GLASGOW NEW YORK TORONTO MELBOURNE WELLINGTON
BOMBAY CALCUTTA MADRAS KARACHI LAHORE DACCA
CAPE TOWN SALISBURY NAIROBI IBADAN ACCRA
KUALA LUMPUR HONG KONG

*Printed in Great Britain
by Richard Clay and Company, Ltd., Bungay, Suffolk*

CONTENTS

AUSTIN CLARKE

TONY CONNOR

CHARLES TOMLINSON

NOTE

Later Poems and *Flight to Africa* by Austin Clarke are published by the Dolmen Press and distributed outside Ireland by Oxford University Press: *With Love Somehow* by Tony Connor, *Seeing is Believing, Versions from Fyodor Tyutchev, A Peopled Landscape,* and *Castilian Ilexes* by Charles Tomlinson, are published by Oxford University Press.

*

AUSTIN CLARKE

*

AISLING

At morning from the coldness of Mount Brandon,
The sail is blowing half-way to the light;
And islands are so small, a man may carry
Their yellow crop in one cart at low tide.
Sadly in thought, I strayed the mountain grass
To hear the breezes following their young
And by the furrow of a stream, I chanced
To find a woman airing in the sun.

Coil of her hair, in cluster and ringlet,
Had brightened round her forehead and those curls—
Closer than she could bind them on a finger—
Were changing gleam and glitter. O she turned
So gracefully aside, I thought her clothes
Were flame and shadow while she slowly walked,
Or that each breast was proud because it rode
The cold air as the wave stayed by the swan.

But knowing her face was fairer than in thought,
I asked of her was she the Geraldine—
Few horsemen sheltered at the steps of water?
Or that Greek woman, lying in a piled room
On tousled purple, whom the household saved,
When frescoes of strange fire concealed the pillar:
The white coin all could spend? Might it be Niav
And was she over wave or from our hills?

'When shadows in wet grass are heavier
Than hay, beside dim wells the women gossip
And by the paler bushes tell the daylight;
But from what bay, uneasy with a shipping
Breeze, have you come?' I said 'O, do you cross
The blue thread and the crimson on the framework,
At darkfall in a house where nobles throng
And the slow oil climbs up into the flame?'

3

'Black and fair strangers leave upon the oar
And there is peace,' she answered. 'Companies
Are gathered in the house that I have known;
Claret is on the board and they are pleased
By story-telling. When the turf is redder
And airy packs of wonder have been told,
My women dance to bright steel that is wed,
Starlike, upon the anvil with one stroke.'

'Shall I, too, find at dark of rain,' I cried,
'Neighbours around a fire cast up by the ocean
And in that shining mansion hear the rise
Of companies, or bide among my own—
Pleasing a noble ear? O must I wander
Without praise, without wine, in rich strange lands?'
But with a smile the secret woman left me.
At morning in the coldness of Mount Brandon.

*

CELIBACY

On a brown isle of Lough Corrib,
When clouds were bare as branch
And water had been thorned
By colder days, I sank
In torment of her side;
But still that woman stayed,
For eye obeys the mind.

Bedraggled in the briar
And grey fire of the nettle,
Three nights, I fell, I groaned
On the flagstone of help
To pluck her from my body;
For servant ribbed with hunger
May climb his rungs to God.

4

Eyelid stood back in sleep,
I saw what seemed an Angel:
Dews dripped from those bright feet.
But, O, I knew the stranger
By her deceit and, tired
All night by tempting flesh,
I wrestled her in hair-shirt.

On pale knees in the dawn,
Parting the straw that wrapped me,
She sank until I saw
The bright roots of her scalp.
She pulled me down to sleep,
But I fled as the Baptist
To thistle and to reed.

The dragons of the Gospel
Are cast by bell and crook;
But fiery as the frost
Or bladed light, she drew
The reeds back, when I fought
The arrow-headed airs
That darken on the water.

*

THE SCHOLAR

SUMMER delights the scholar
With knowledge and reason.
Who is happy in hedgerow
Or meadow as he is?

Paying no dues to the parish,
He argues in logic
And has no care of cattle
But a satchel and stick.

The showery airs grow softer,
He profits from his ploughland
For the share of the schoolmen
Is a pen in hand.

When mid-day hides the reaping,
He sleeps by a river
Or comes to the stone plain
Where the saints live.

But in winter by the big fires,
The ignorant hear his fiddle,
And he battles on the chessboard,
As the land lords bid him.

*

MARTHA BLAKE

BEFORE the day is everywhere
And the timid warmth of sleep
Is delicate on limb, she dares
The silence of the street
Until the double bells are thrown back
For Mass and echoes bound
In the chapel yard, O then her soul
Makes bold in the arms of sound.

But in the shadow of the nave
Her well-taught knees are humble,
She does not see through any saint
That stands in the sun
With veins of lead, with painful crown;
She waits that dreaded coming,
When all the congregation bows
And none may look up.

6

The word is said, the Word sent down,
The miracle is done
Beneath those hands that have been rounded
Over the embodied cup,
And with a few, she leaves her place
Kept by an east-filled window
And kneels at the communion rail
Starching beneath her chin.

She trembles for the Son of Man,
While the priest is murmuring
What she can scarcely tell, her heart
Is making such a stir;
But when he picks a particle
And she puts out her tongue,
That joy is the glittering of candles
And benediction sung.

Her soul is lying in the Presence
Until her senses, one
By one, desiring to attend her,
Come as for feast and run
So fast to share the sacrament,
Her mouth must mother them:
'Sweet tooth grow wise, lip, gum be gentle,
I touch a purple hem.'

Afflicted by that love she turns
To multiply her praise,
Goes over all the foolish words
And finds they are the same;
But now she feels within her breast
Such calm that she is silent,
For soul can never be immodest
Where body may not listen.

On a holy day of obligation
I saw her first in prayer,
But mortal eye had been too late
For all that thought could dare.
The flame in heart is never grieved
That pride and intellect
Were cast below, when God revealed
A heaven for this earth.

So to begin the common day
She needs a miracle,
Knowing the safety of angels
That see her home again,
Yet ignorant of all the rest,
The hidden grace that people
Hurrying to business
Look after in the street.

*

THE STRAYING STUDENT

On a holy day when sails were blowing southward,
A bishop sang the Mass at Inishmore,
Men took one side, their wives were on the other
But I heard the woman coming from the shore :
And wild in despair my parents cried aloud
For they saw the vision draw me to the doorway.

Long had she lived in Rome when Popes were bad,
The wealth of every age she makes her own,
Yet smiled on me in eager admiration,
And for a summer taught me all I know,
Banishing shame with her great laugh that rang
As if a pillar caught it back alone.

I learned the prouder counsel of her throat,
My mind was growing bold as light in Greece;
And when in sleep her stirring limbs were shown,
I blessed the noonday rock that knew no tree:
And for an hour the mountain was her throne,
Although her eyes were bright with mockery.

They say I was sent back from Salamanca
And failed in logic, but I wrote her praise
Nine times upon a college wall in France.
She laid her hand at darkfall on my page
That I might read the heavens in a glance
And I knew every star the Moors have named.

Awake or in my sleep, I have no peace now,
Before the ball is struck, my breath has gone,
And yet I tremble lest she may deceive me
And leave me in this land, where every woman's son
Must carry his own coffin and believe,
In dread, all that the clergy teach the young.

*

PENAL LAW

Burn Ovid with the rest. Lovers will find
A hedge-school for themselves and learn by heart
All that the clergy banish from the mind,
When hands are joined and head bows in the dark.

*

THE ENVY OF POOR LOVERS

Pity poor lovers who may not do what they please
With their kisses under a hedge, before a raindrop
Unhouses it; and astir from wretched centuries,
Bramble and briar remind them of the saints.

Her envy is the curtain seen at night-time,
Happy position that could change her name.
His envy—clasp of the married whose thoughts can be alike,
Whose nature flows without the blame or shame.

Lying in the grass as if it were a sin
To move, they hold each other's breath, tremble,
Ready to share that ancient dread—kisses begin
Again—of Ireland keeping company with them.

Think, children, of institutions mured above
Your ignorance, where every look is veiled,
State-paid to snatch away the folly of poor lovers
For whom, it seems, the sacraments have failed.

*

ANCIENT LIGHTS

When all of us wore smaller shoes
And knew the next world better than
The knots we broke, I used to hurry
On missions of my own to Capel
Street, Bolton Street and Granby Row
To see what man has made. But darkness
Was roomed with fears. Sleep, stripped by woes
I had been taught, beat door, leaped landing,
Lied down the banisters of naught.

Being sent to penance, come Saturday,
I shuffled slower than my sins should.
My fears were candle-spiked at side-shrines,
Rays lengthened them in stained-glass. Confided
To night again, my grief bowed down,
Heard hand on shutter-knob. Did I
Take pleasure, when alone—how much—
In a bad thought, immodest look
Or worse, unnecessary touch?

Closeted in the confessional,
I put on flesh, so many years
Were added to my own, attempted
In vain to keep Dominican
As much i' the dark as I was, mixing
Whispered replies with his low words;
Then shuddered past the crucifix,
The feet so hammered, daubed-on blood-drip,
Black with lip-scrimmage of the damned.

Once as I crept from the church-steps,
Beside myself, the air opened
On purpose. Nature read in a flutter
An evening lesson above my head.
Atwirl beyond the leadings, corbels,
A cage-bird came among sparrows
(The moral inescapable)
Plucked, roof-mired, all in mad bits. O
The pizzicato of its wires!

Goodness of air can be proverbial:
That day, by the kerb at Rutland Square,
A bronze bird fabled out of trees,
Mailing the spearheads of the railings,
Sparrow at nails. I hailed the skies
To save the tiny dropper, found
Appetite gone. A child of clay
Had blustered it away. Pity
Could raise some littleness from dust.

What Sunday clothes can change us now
Or humble orders in black and white?
Stinking with centuries the act
Of thought. So think, man, as Augustine
Did, dread the ink-bespattered ex-monk,
And keep your name. No, let me abandon
Night's jakes. Self-persecuted of late
Among the hatreds of rent Europe,
Poetry burns at a different stake.

Still, still I remember aweful downpour
Cabbing Mountjoy Street, spun loneliness
Veiling almost the Protestant church,
Two backyards from my very home.
I dared to shelter at locked door.
There, walled by heresy, my fears
Were solved. I had absolved myself:
Feast-day effulgence, as though I gained
For life a plenary indulgence.

The sun came out, new smoke flew up,
The gutters of the Black Church rang
With services. Waste water mocked
The ballcocks: down-pipes sparrowing,
And all around the spires of Dublin
Such swallowing in the air, such cowling
To keep high offices pure: I heard
From shore to shore, the iron gratings
Take half our heavens with a roar.

*

ABBEY THEATRE FIRE

PRIDE made of Yeats a rhetorician.
He would have called them knave or clown,
The playwright, poet, politician,
Who pull his Abbey Theatre down.
Scene-dock and wardrobe choked with rage,
When warriors in helmets saved
The auditorium and stage.
Forgetting our age, he waved and raved
Of Art and thought her Memory's daughter.
Those firemen might have spared their water.

*

MEDICAL MISSIONARY OF MARY

ONE blowy morning, Sister Michael,
A student of midwifery,
Fell, handlebarring from her cycle,
Her habit twisted around a pedal:
She suffered bruises on her riff,
Serious injury to the spine
And so, in hope of miracle,
Was brought, a stretcher case, to Lourdes
Out of the blue, above the shrining
Of snowy peaks: unchosen, uncured
Although she had made novena, kissed
The relics: worse than ever, came back
By London, lying on her back,
Saw there, thank Heaven, a specialist
And now is on the recovery list.

*

MARTHA BLAKE AT FIFTY-ONE

EARLY, each morning, Martha Blake
    Walked, angeling the road,
To Mass in the Church of the Three Patrons.
    Sanctuary lamp glowed
And the clerk halo'ed the candles
    On the High Altar. She knelt
Illumined. In gold-hemmed alb,
    The priest intoned. Wax melted.

Waiting for daily Communion, bowed head
    At rail, she hears a murmur.
Latin is near. In a sweet cloud
    That cherub'd, all occurred.

13

The voice went by. To her pure thought,
  Body was a distress
And soul, a sigh. Behind her denture,
  Love lay, a helplessness.

Then, slowly walking after Mass
  Down Rathgar Road, she took out
Her Yale key, put a match to gas-ring,
  Half filled a saucepan, cooked
A fresh egg lightly, with tea, brown bread.
  Soon, taking off her blouse
And skirt, she rested, pressing the Crown
  Of Thorns until she drowsed.

In her black hat, stockings, she passed
  Nylons to a nearby shop
And purchased, daily, with downcast eyes,
  Fillet of steak or a chop.
She simmered it on a low jet,
  Having a poor appetite,
Yet never for an hour felt better
  From dilatation, tightness.

She suffered from dropped stomach, heartburn,
  Scalding, water-brash
And when she brought her wind up, turning
  Red with the weight of mashed
Potato, mint could not relieve her.
  In vain her many belches,
For all below was swelling, heaving
  Wamble, gurgle, squelch.

She lay on the sofa with legs up,
  A decade on her lip,
At four o'clock, taking a cup
  Of lukewarm water, sip
By sip, but still her daily food
  Repeated and the bile
Tormented her. In a blue hood,
  The Virgin sadly smiled.

When she looked up, the Saviour showed
    His Heart, daggered with flame
And, from the mantel-shelf, St. Joseph
    Bent, disapproving. Vainly
She prayed for in the whatnot corner,
    The new Pope was frowning. Night
And day, dull pain, as in her corns,
    Recounted every bite.

She thought of St. Teresa, floating
    On motes of a sunbeam,
Carmelite with scatterful robes,
    Surrounded by demons,
Small black boys in their skin. She gaped
    At Hell: a muddy passage
That led to nothing, queer in shape,
    A cupboard closely fastened.

Sometimes, the walls of the parlour
    Would fade away. No plod
Of feet, rattle of van, in Garville
    Road. Soul now gone abroad
Where saints, like medieval serfs,
    Had laboured. Great sun-flower shone.
Our Lady's Chapel was borne by seraphs,
    Three leagues beyond Ancona.

High towns of Italy, the plain
    Of France, were known to Martha
As she read in a holy book. The sky-blaze
    Nooned at Padua,
Marble grotto of Bernadette.
    Rose-scatterers. New saints
In tropical Africa where the tsetse
    Fly probes, the forest taints.

Teresa had heard the Lutherans
   Howling on red-hot spit,
And grill, men who had searched for truth
   Alone in Holy Writ.
So Martha, fearful of flame lashing
   Those heretics, each instant,
Never dealt in the haberdashery
   Shop, owned by two Protestants.

In ambush of night, an angel wounded
   The Spaniard to the heart
With iron tip on fire. Swooning
   With pain and bliss as a dart
Moved up and down within her bowels
   Quicker, quicker, each cell
Sweating as if rubbed up with towels,
   Her spirit rose and fell.

St. John of the Cross, her friend in prison
   Awaits the bridal night,
Paler than lilies, his wizened skin
   Flowers. In fifths of flight,
Senses beyond seraphic thought,
   In that divinest clasp,
Enfolding of kisses that cauterize,
   Yield to the soul-spasm.

Cunning in body had come to hate
   All this and stirred by mischief
Haled Martha from heaven. Heart palpitates
   And terror in her stiffens.
Heart misses one beat, two . . . flutters . . . stops.
   Her ears are full of sound.
Half fainting, she stares at the grandfather clock
   As if it were overwound.

The fit had come. Ill-natured flesh
  Despised her soul. No bending
Could ease rib. Around her heart, pressure
  Of wind grew worse. Again,
Again, armchaired without relief
  She eructated, phlegm
In mouth, forget the woe, the grief,
  Foretold at Bethlehem.

Tired of the same faces, side-altars,
  She went to the Carmelite Church
At Johnson's Court, confessed her faults,
  There, once a week, purchased
Tea, butter in Chatham St. The pond
  In St. Stephen's Green was grand.
She watched the seagulls, ducks, black swan,
  Went home by the 15 tram.

Her beads in hand, Martha became
  A member of the Third Order,
Saved from long purgatorial pain,
  Brown habit and white cord
Her own when cerges had been lit
  Around her coffin. She got
Ninety-five pounds on loan for her bit
  Of clay in the common plot.

Often she thought of a quiet sick-ward,
  Nuns, with delicious ways,
Consoling the miserable : quick
  Tea, toast on trays. Wishing
To rid themselves of her, kind neighbours
  Sent for the ambulance,
Before her brother and sister could hurry
  To help her. Big gate clanged.

No medical examination
    For the new patient. Doctor
Had gone to Cork on holidays.
    Telephone sprang. Hall-clock
Proclaimed the quarters. Clatter of heels
    On tiles. Corridor, ward,
A-whirr with the electric cleaner,
    The creak of window cord.

She could not sleep at night. Feeble
    And old, two women raved
And cried to God. She held her beads.
    O how could she be saved?
The hospital had this and that rule.
    Day-chill unshuttered. Nun, with
Thermometer in reticule,
    Went by. The women mumbled.

Mother Superior believed
    That she was obstinate, self-willed.
Sisters ignored her, hands-in-sleeves,
    Beside a pantry shelf
Or counting pillow-case, soiled sheet.
    They gave her purgatives.
Soul-less, she tottered to the toilet.
    Only her body lived.

Wasted by colitis, refused
    The daily sacrament
By regulation, forbidden use
    Of bed-pan, when meals were sent up,
Behind a screen, she lay, shivering,
    Unable to eat. The soup
Was greasy, mutton, beef or liver,
    Cold. Kitchen has no scruples.

18

The Nuns had let the field in front
    As an Amusement Park,
Merry-go-round, a noisy month, all
    Heltering-skeltering at darkfall,
Mechanical music, dipper, hold-tights,
    Rifle-crack, crash of dodgems.
The ward, godless with shadow, lights,
    How could she pray to God?

Unpitied, wasting with diarrhoea
    And the constant strain,
Poor Child of Mary with one idea,
    She ruptured a small vein,
Bled inwardly to jazz. No priest
    Came. She had been anointed
Two days before, yet knew no peace:
    Her last breath, disappointed.

*

UNMARRIED MOTHERS

In the Convent of the Sacred Heart,
The Long Room has been decorated
Where a Bishop can dine off golden plate:
As Oriental Potentate.
Girls, who will never wheel a go-cart,
Cook, sew, wash, dig, milk cows, clean stables
And, twice a day, giving their babes
The teat, herdlike, yield milk that cost
Them dearly, when their skirts were tossed up
Above their haunches. Hook or zip
Has warded them at Castlepollard.
Luckier girls, on board a ship,
Watch new hope spraying from the bollard.

*

19

JAPANESE PRINT

BOTH skyed
In south-west wind beyond
Poplar and fir-tree, swallow,
Heron, almost collide,
Swerve
With a rapid
Dip of wing, flap,
Each in an opposite curve,
Fork-tail, long neck outstretched
And feet. All happened
Above my head. The pair
Was disappearing. Say I
Had seen, half hint, a sketch on
Rice-coloured air,
Sharako, Hokusai!

*

A STRONG WIND

ALL day a strong wind blew
Across the green and brown from Kerry.
The leaves hurrying, two
By three, over the road, collected
In chattering groups. New berry
Dipped with old branch. Careful insects
Flew low behind their hedges.
Held back by her pretty petticoat,
Butterfly struggled. A bit of
Paper, on which a schoolgirl had written
'Máire loves Jimmy', jumped up
Into a tree. Tapping in haste,
The wind was telegraphing, hundreds
Of miles. All Ireland raced.

*

THE EIGHTH WONDER OF IRELAND

I

GIRALDUS CAMBRENSIS recounted the seven wonders
Of Ireland. Hot hedge, impenetrable pale
On fire, up, down, around, between and under,
Protecting the holy virgins from our male
Intrusion at Kildare. Bell, with a stoop,
Hobbling in round of mercy from the belfry
At Fore. Delight of priest and deacon, stoop
That brims with wine for daily Mass. Steep, self-
descending, ten-mile-sounding, ship-devouring,
Green, glassy, walling Whirlpool. Bull-man
Mounting in turn twelve crummies, glowering
In field. Cross in the parish of Rathoath
That spoke against false witnesses on oath.
Tincture of island clay that cures the bite
Of reptile, adder, lessens ayen-bite.

II

To the seven wonders of Ireland, add an eighth.
Thrones and Dominions have changed our copybooks.
Crooked is straight, upside is down, pothooks
Are hangers, good is bad now, pity, cruel,
Free medicine, school-milk, contrary to Faith;
The old, the sick, cannot have soup or fuel,
Parents, who anguish vainly to support
Their infants, are robbed of them, unhomed in Court,
Pelfing is grace, substance of self, a wraith.

*

COCK AND HEN
After the Irish

A COCK and hen strayed on their travels
From Birr to Navan, until one Thursday,
They drooped their tails in a prison-cell
At Sligo. Bar, bench, jurymen heard
That scandalous pair. Case was dismissed,
Struck from the list, so they went to the grazings
Of William MacShane. Near rock, cloud, mist,
They fed on fraughans, slept in a hayfield.

'You should have seen my cock as he reached
From his horse,' the Hen said, 'at the big fair
Of Galway, daring all, his breeches
So finely stitched, gold watch with figures,
Rapier hilt and spurs, new suit,
Gauntlets that fitted him, laced hat,
He rode, he dandied with polished top-boots
Of Spanish leather, crop in hand.

'I came to Tom Hood's,' the Cock said, 'hens picking,
No bantam or chick with them, I rustled
The straw and bustled beneath a half rick,
Then trod the layers quickly, hustling
Them off and lusted on the dung-hill,
Doors open. "Kill that new cock, Mary,
You've time to spare." She caught, wrung, weighed me,
Is it my fate to be plucked bare?'

'My grief,' the Hen sobbed at night on her roost,
'Bed-partner, who used to tread me gladly,
My children's father is boiled. His juices
Cling to the pot. Tail tingles, lonely, sad,
Feather and bone. A young Spring widow,
I snap my bill at those who shamed him,
Cursing the women at Ballinrobe,
For grain is chaff, without my game-cock.'

*

FORGET ME NOT

Up the hill,
Hurry me not;
Down the hill,
Worry me not;
On the level,
Spare me not,
In the stable,
Forget me not.

Trochaic dimeter, amphimacer
And choriamb, with hyper catalexis,
Grammatical inversion, springing of double
Rhyme. So we learned to scan all, analyse
Lyric and ode, elegy, anonymous patter,
For what is song itself but substitution?
Let classical terms unroll, with a flourish, the scroll
Of baccalaureate.

                Coleridge had picked
That phrase for us—*vergiss-mein-nicht,* emblem
Of love and friendship, delicate sentiments.
Forget-me-nots, forget-me-nots:
Blue, sunny-eyed young hopefuls! He left a nosegay,
A keepsake for Kate Greenaway.

                      Child climbed
Into the trap; the pony started quick
As fly to a flick and Uncle John began
Our work-a-day, holiday jingle.

                      Up the hill.
Hurry me not.
                Down the hill,
Worry me not.
                  Verse came like that, simple
As join-hands, yet ambiguous, lesson
Implied, a flower-puzzle in final verb
And negative. All was personification
As we drove on: invisibility

23

Becoming audible. A kindness spoke,
Assumed the god; consensus everywhere
In County Dublin. Place-names, full of Sunday,
Stepaside, Pass-if-you-can Lane, Hole in the Wall.
Such foliage in the Dargle hid Lovers Leap,
We scarcely heard the waters fall-at-all.
Often the open road to Celbridge: we came back
By Lucan Looks Lovely, pulled in at the Strawberry Beds,
Walked up the steep of Knockmaroon. Only
The darkness could complete our rounds. The pony
Helped, took the bit. Coat-buttoned up, well-rugg'd,
I drowsed till the clatter of city sets, warning
Of echoes around St. Mary's Place, woke me;
But I was guarded by medal, scapular
And the *Agnus Dei* next my skin, passing
That Protestant Church. Night shirt, warm manger, confusion
Of premise, creed; I sank through mysteries
To our oblivion.

Ora pro nobis

Ora pro me.

                    'Gee up', 'whoa', 'steady', 'hike',
'Hike ow'a that.' Rough street-words, cheerful, impatient:
The hearers knew their own names as well. Horses,
Men, going together to daily work; dairy
Cart, baker's van, slow dray, quick grocery
Deliveries. Street-words, the chaff in them.
Suddenly in Mountjoy Street, at five o'clock
Yes, five in the evening, work rhymed for a minute with
    sport.
Church-echoing wheel-rim, roof-beat, tattle of harness
Around the corner of St. Mary's Place:
Cabs, outside cars, the drivers unranked in race
For tips; their horses eager to compete,
With spark and hubbub, greet with their own heat
Galway Express that puffed to Broadstone Station.
They held that Iron Horse in great esteem
Yet dared the metamorphosis of steam.
Soon they were back again. I ran to watch

As Uncle John in elegant light tweeds
Drove smartly by on his outside car, talking
Over his shoulder to a straight-up fare
Or two, coaxing by name his favourite mare;
The best of jarvies, his sarcastic wit
Checked by a bridle rein; and he enlarged
My mind with two Victorian words. Grown-ups
Addressed him as Town Councillor, Cab
And Car Proprietor!
                  Horse-heads above me,
Below me. Happy on tram top, I looked down
On plaited manes, alighted safely, caught
Sidelong near kerb, perhaps, affectionate glance
As I passed a blinker. Much to offend the pure:
Let-down or drench, the sparrows pecking at fume,
The scavengers with shovel, broom. But, O
When horse fell down, pity was there: we saw
Such helplessness, girth buckled, no knack in knee,
Half-upturned legs—big hands that couldn't unclench
A parable, pride or the like, rough-shod,
Or goodness put in irons, then, soul uplifted
Bodily; traffic no longer interrupted.
Strength broadened in narrow ways. Champions went by,
Guinness's horses from St. James's Gate:
Their brasses clinked, yoke, collar shone at us:
Light music while they worked. Side-streets, alleys
Beyond St. Patrick's, floats unloading, country
Colt, town hack, hay-cart, coal-bell. Often the whip-crack,
The lash of rain. Hand-stitch in the numb of pain
At school. Religious orders plied the strap
On us, but never on themselves. Each day, too,
Justice tore off her bandage in Mountjoy Street.
The Black Maria passed, van o' the poor.
Weeks, months clung to those bars, cursed, or stared, mute.
Children in rags ran after that absenting,
Did double time to fetlocks. Solemnity
For all; the mournful two or four with plumes,
Hooves blackened to please your crape. The funerals

Go faster now. Our Christianity
Still catching up with All is Vanity.

Nevertheless
Nature had learned to share our worldliness,
Well-pleased to keep with man the colours in hide,
Dappling much, glossing the chestnut, sunshading the bays,
To grace those carriage wheels, that *vis-à-vis*
In the Park. Let joy cast off a trace, for once,
High-stepping beyond the Phoenix Monument
In the long ago of British Rule, I saw
With my own eyes a white horse that unfabled
The Unicorn.
            Mechanized vehicles:
Horse-power by handle-turn. My Uncle John
Lost stable companions, drivers, all. Though poor,
He kept his last mare out on grass. They aged
Together. At twenty-one, I thought it right
And proper.
           How could I know that greed
Spreads quicker than political hate? No need
Of propaganda. Good company, up and down
The ages, gone: the trick of knife left, horse cut
To serve man. All the gentling, custom of mind
And instinct, close affection, done with. The unemployed
Must go. Dead or ghosted by froths, we ship them
Abroad. Foal, filly, farm pony, bred for slaughter:
What are they now but hundredweights of meat?
A double trade. Greed with a new gag of mercy
Grants happy release in our whited abbatoirs.
'Gentlemen, businessmen, kill on the spot! O
That,' exclaim the good, 'should be your motto.
Combine in a single trade all profits, save
Sensitive animals from channelling wave,
Continental docking, knackering down.
We dread bad weather, zig-zag, tap of Morse.'
Well-meaning fools, who only pat the horse
That looks so grand on our Irish half-crown.

I've more to say—

Men of Great Britain

Openly share with us the ploughtail, the field-spoil,
Trucking in Europe what we dare not broil
At home.

Herodotus condemned

Hippophagy.

And Pliny, also.
Besieged towns

Denied it.

Stare now at Pegasus. The blood

Of the Medusa weakens in him.

Yet all the world

Was hackneyed once—those horses o' the sun,
Apollo's car, centaurs in Thessaly.
Too many staves have splintered the toy
That captured Troy. The Hippocrene is stale.
Dark ages; Latin rotted, came up from night-soil,
New rush of words; thought mounted them. Trappings
Of palfrey, sword-kiss of chivalry, high song
Of grammar. Men pick the ribs of Rosinante
In restaurants now. Horse-shoe weighs in with saddle
Of meat.

Horseman, the pass-word, courage shared

With lace, steel, buff.

Wars regimented

Haunches together. Cities move by in motor
Cars, charging the will. I hear in the lateness of Empires,
A neighing, man's cry in engines. No peace, yet,
Poor draggers of artillery.

The moon

Eclipsed: I stood on the Rock of Cashel, saw dimly
Carved on the royal arch of Cormac's Chapel
Sign of the Sagittary, turned my back
On all that Celtic Romanesque; thinking
Of older story and legend, how Cuchullain,
Half man, half god-son, tamed the elemental
Coursers: dear comrades: how at his death

The Gray of Macha laid her mane upon his breast
And wept.
                          I struggled down
From paleness of limestone.
                                        Too much historied
Land, wrong in policies, armings, hope in prelates
At courts abroad! Rags were your retribution,
Hedge schools, a visionary knowledge in verse
That hid itself. The rain-drip cabin'd the dream
Of foreign aid . . . Democracy at last.
White horses running through the European mind
Of the First Consul. Our heads were cropped like his.
New brow; old imagery. A Gaelic poet,
Pitch-capped in the Rebellion of '98.
Called this Republic in an allegory
The Slight Red Steed.

                          Word-loss is now our gain:
Put mare to stud. Is Ireland any worse
Than countries that fly-blow the map, rattle the sky,
Drop down from it? Tipsters respect our grand sires,
Thorough-breds, jumpers o' the best.
Our grass still makes a noble show, and the roar
Of money cheers us at the winning post.
So pack tradition in the meat-sack, Boys,
Write off the epitaph of Yeats.

                          I'll turn
To jogtrot, pony bell, say my first lesson:

> *Up the hill,*
> *Hurry me not;*
> *Down the hill,*
> *Worry me not;*
> *On the level,*
> *Spare me not,*
> *In the stable,*
> *Forget me not.*
>
> *Forget me not.*

*

THE PLOT

So, in accordance with the plot,
MacDonagh, Plunkett, Pearse, were shot.
Campbell dropped dead in a mountainy spot,
Stephens, lifting the chamber pot.
O Conaire went, a ragged sot.
Higgins was coffined in a clot.
Twice-warned, when must I join our lot?

*

BEYOND THE PALE

Pleasant, my Nora, on a May morning to drive
Along the roads of Ireland, going south,
See Wicklow hilling from car window, down
And pinewood, buttercupping grass, field-wire,
The shelves of hawthorn, konker bud on chestnut
Bulging with sun-shadowings, brook-lime,
The yellow iris-curl, flower o' the cress
And Slaney gliding around a sandy nook
Through flaggeries into the narrower falls,
Beyond the mills with rusty flange, cogwheel
And moss of the sluice, hear the jackdawing,
Yet sad to speed from the inn, along the bogland
Where State machines are cutting turf for miles
That furnaces may stop the centuries
Of turbary, put out an ancient fire.
Hardly a living soul upon these roads:
Both young and old hasten to quit the dung,
The chicken-run, lean-to, sty, thistle blow
Of fields once measured by buckshot, midnight bung.
Foreign factories in towns employ
Chattering girls: few levers for a boy.

29

Pleasant to climb the Rock of Dunamace,
A goat upon a crag, a falcon swerving
Above: heraldic shield of air, chevroned
With brown and *or*: later the rounded walls
And bastion were raised beside the squat
Keep: they could bounce away the cannon balls.
The culdees knew each drumlin, sun-thatched spot,
By rising road, fern-corner, come to Wolf Hill:
Men working underground, tap anthracite.
Stacks are shed-high. The heatherland is chill.
That earth is black except for a blue-white image
Seen far, a statue of the Blessed Virgin
Beside the road, a solitary hymn
To a great owner. Beneath the pious verge
Of the mine-hill is his public-house, his sign—
The Swan, beside a holy statuette:
Nearby his factory with store of drain-pipes,
Trim row by row, a Sacred Heart beset
By glass of shrine and on the outer wall
Behold a plaque in loving memory
Of Joseph Fleming, Irish patriot,
Industrialist and good employer. Night-stealing,
He fought the English, ready with rifle shot
To serve his country.
                                   Higher still.

                                         Pleasant,
My love, upon Mount Leinster, passing the spruce,
Fir, pine plantations, as a red-brown pheasant
Comes bustling up from heather, bends the juicy
Grass-stalk, to scan the middle plain below,
A map of cloud, the fields of beetroot penned;
Dividing sea.

            Signpost to Kilkenny:
The Georgian almshouses, tree-pent, College
Where Congreve, Swift, had learned about addition,
The passage steps between the danks of wall,
Martins high up at the city bridge,

Swallows, their black-and-white playing at tig.
Along the River Nore, chasing the midgets
Where, biding in the sedge, the young trout nab
Their share. Behind the Thorsel, the Black Abbey,
A street of little shops, a painted set,
Drop-scene for Harlequin. Embattled might:
Norman Cathedral with its monuments,
Marble of tablet and recumbent knights
In effigy beside obedient wives, knees bent.
A black dog flamed, leg up. Dame Kyttler scoffed there
At Mass—her house is now a betting office—
Too long at night she had been irked by the Belt
Of Chastity. So, stripping to the pelt,
Leftwise, she wrote the Tetragrammaton.
The Devil came, volumed in smoke from a gorge
Beyond the Caucasus, breakneck upon
Foul wind. She wanted topsy-turvy orgy
And, taking her by the loblongs, Fiery dawdled,
Unpadlocked her with ice-cold key. Melled, twisting
In exquisite pain, she lay with open wards
While her companion, Petronella, was kissed
Introrsely by Black Fitzjames, knighted in hell.
He picked her keyhole with his skeleton,
Fire-freezing through her pelvis, but she missed
The bliss, though he was cap-à-pie as Guelf.
Soon afterwards, they say, that demon sired
The black cats of Kilkenny. They fought for scales
Of market fish, left nothing but their own tails
And their descendants never sit by the fire-side.
Disedifying Latin, clerical tales
Corrupt us.

            Only one poet, Coventry
Patmore, who wived three times, has written of love
In matrimony, pulled the curtain back, showed
From post to post, the hush of featherbed,
Lace counterpane, mahogany commode:
And here from hoop and bustle, petticoats, pleating,

Long drawers, to eiderdown, our Fanny glowed;
Too cushiony, too gross, in such an abode
For Psyche.
                    Our convert, right or wrong,
                                        believed
That in the midnight transport, every spouse
Knew Heaven, like us, by the oriental spice.
So Virtue, blushing at a little vice,
Turned down the incandescent mantle, unbloused
The globes of sin.

                              'This, this, is telling secrets.
Burn every page,' wrote Gerard Manley Hopkins.
'Only upon that morning when the skin hops
To bone and sinew again, must Truth be published.'
Then shall the Unmentionable be purified,
Pearl, ruby, amethyst, all grace inside.'

So, turning west, we drive to Borrisokane.
The Misses O'Leary own a small hotel
And shop there, have for pet, a middle-aged hen.
She clucks and picks all day, is never fluttered.
I see her twice a year, yes, know her well,
And spoon an egg of hers, boiled lightly, buttered,
At breakfast, scrape it to the very shell.

Delightful to be in Tipperary, greenest
Of all the counties, drive by coltsfoot stream
And spinney, gearing up to Silvermines
Forgetting that Europe closed the mountain till
Or hear the haggling at a monthly market,
Farmers go by and women with fat thighs,
The milk-cans clanking on their little carts, to
Co-operative creameries, light smoke,
Ruffle of separators: come to byways
Where sawmills whirr with easy belt, see glow
Of welding in forges, hurry to Lough Derg.
May-fly is nymphlike there, pearling her veils,

Soon is bewinged. The shadow of a berg
Is greening, paling. Dappers hear about them
The noise of carburettors, modern roar
Of water-skiing as the speedboats clap on
The spray. Young one, legs apart, toes out,
Classical in her scantlet of bright costume,
Our Naiad, offering wet little posy
To Nereus while summery splashes, tossed
By board or skip of rope, go bottoming,
Head over heels.

             Storm out of the South-West
From Banagher, Clonfert, across the flats,
Leaf-crushes of rain, the darkness coming faster.
The barges are rotting at wharves. Canal Hotel,
Where shivering children peep from the broken panes,
At Shannon Harbour, now a tenement.
The lake-winds whistle, dip-dipping the slenderers.
In runs of air, the saltness is besprent.
At Gallerus, the pale Atlantic rages.
Bad weather, hard times, known to the Ancient Crow
Of Achill, flapping out of the earth-brown pages
Of manuscripts, the Stag of Leiterlone
Uncragging, Fintan, half-way from transmigration,
A roaming salmon, where billows dredge the shingle.

Now, after a century of rags, young girl
With skin the insolent have fondled, Earl
And settler in his turn, the Hag of Dingle
Is stretching. Eire, clamant with piety,
Remembering the old mythology.

*

TONY CONNOR

*

TONY CONNOR

I DO not intend to contribute
a single line, any half-heard
snatch of mystery
to the street's chronicle.
I am deaf among men;
I am dumb among women;
I am the prince of never-there,
the master of winter.

I have no knowledge to offer
about the marriage bed,
nor am I able to say
where, or why important
decisions were made
affecting the lives
of all who heard them
and many more who did not.

I will not pretend an ability
to judge character from faces;
darkness frightens me
and I am apprehensive in sunlight.
Nevertheless,
mine was the bland smile,
the fur coat of incomprehension
in the catastrophe.

When the trek ended, frustrated
by the abattoir wall,
and the disgusted others
started rewinding the string,
I was in the chip shop
ordering fourpenn'orth.
I had not come all that way
for nothing.

On certain nights I have discerned
complicated patterns
in smudged penumbras,
but have never missed my supper.
The voices from alleys
—loving or hating—
I have accepted as part
of a wholesome definition.

You will appreciate my reluctance
to give you directions:
my inability to reach
the homes of others
is widely known—
although one of my hobbies
is studying maps
in the front room.

Finally, let me assure those
who imagine me lending a willing ear,
that my lopsided appearance
is congenital,
and should not be interpreted
as a leaning
towards anything
other than the ground.

*

THE CROFT

THE croft, shadowed between houses,
blotchy with grass like fading bruises,
had hardly ground to be called croft,
being no more than an unclaimed cleft

in a grubby, once stately, row
of four-window fronts done in stucco.
Shut like a world in a glass ball
this is where childhood befell

whatever it is that's stepped on
into my moving imagination.
Name, purpose, family face,
were vivid daydreams of that place,

where, ear cocked to the sour earth
and the scavenging rats' scratch beneath
in caved cellars, my mind embodied
populous otherwheres to be studied;

a God who, if he cared to come,
might broken-glass-top wall that kingdom,
or (since an old Jew, who retailed fish
there before his shop was demolished)

might sell the burst mattress, the frames
of bike and umbrella, and the bones
buried by dogs, even the mind
that summoned him from the back of the wind.

The real abides; the poem finds it.
By instinct: cat or dog-wit
of sniff and sixth sense, the poem
follows its own secret way home.

Time, that had shored, crumbles. The years,
their accreted populous otherwheres,
vanish, and I alone am left,
I and the poem and the croft

too close for distinction. Rats beneath
scurry and squeak; from his burst mouth
the ever-present God speaks—
innocuous rhetoric of wet kapok.

*

ELEGY FOR ALFRED HUBBARD

HUBBARD is dead, the old plumber;
who will mend our burst pipes now,
the tap that has dripped all the summer,
testing the sink's overflow?

No other like him. Young men with knowledge
of new techniques, theories from books,
may better his work straight from college,
but who will challenge his squint-eyed looks

in kitchen, bathroom, under floorboards,
rules of thumb which were often wrong;
seek as erringly stopcocks in cupboards,
or make a job last half as long?

He was a man who knew the ginnels,
alleyways, streets—the whole district,
family secrets, minor annals,
time-honoured fictions fused to fact.

Seventy years of gossip muttered
under his cap, his tufty thatch,
so that his talk was slow and clotted,
hard to follow, and too much.

As though nothing fell, none vanished,
and time were the maze of Cheetham Hill,
in which the dead—with jobs unfinished—
waited to hear him ring the bell.

For much he never got round to doing,
but meant to, when weather bucked up,
or worsened, or when his pipe was drawing,
or when he'd finished this cup.

I thought time, he forgot so often,
had forgotten him, but here's Death's pomp
over his house, and by the coffin
the son who will inherit his blowlamp,

tools, workshop, cart, and cornet
(pride of Cheetham Prize Brass Band),
and there's his mourning widow, Janet,
stood at the gate he'd promised to mend.

Soon he will make his final journey;
shaved and silent, strangely trim,
with never a pause to talk to any-
body : how arrow-like, for him!

In St. Mark's Church, whose dismal tower
he pointed and painted when a lad,
they will sing his praises amidst flowers
while, somewhere, a cellar starts to flood,

and the housewife banging his front-door knocker
is not surprised to find him gone,
and runs for Thwaite, who's a better worker,
and sticks at a job until it's done.

*

APOLOGUE

HAVING a fine new suit,
and no invitations,
I slept in my new suit
hoping to induce
a dream of fair women.

41

And did indeed: the whole night long,
implored by naked
beauty—pink on white linen—
I struggled to remove
my fine new suit.

At dawn I awoke, blear-eyed;
sweating beneath encumbering rags.

*

THE BURGLARY

It's two o'clock now; somebody's pausing in the street
to turn up his collar. The night's black: distraught
with chimney-toppling wind and harsh rain—
see, the wet's soaking in on the end-gable,
and the frothing torrent, overspilling the broken drain,

accosts the pavement with incoherent babble.
There is the house we want: how easy to burgle,
with its dark trees, and the lawn set back from the road;
the owners will be in bed now—the old couple;
you've got the position of the safe?—Yes, I know the code.

The cock's going mad up there on the church steeple;
the wind's enormous—will it ever stifle;
still, its noise, and the rain's are with us, I daresay,
they'll cover what we make, if we go careful
round by the greenhouse, and in at the back way.

Here's the broken sash I mentioned;—no need to be fearful,
watch how I do it: these fingers are facile
with the practice I've had on worse nights than this.
I tell you, the whole thing's going to be a doddle:
the way I've got it worked out, we can't miss.

Although, God knows, most things turn out a muddle,
and it only confuses more to look for a moral.
Wherever I've been the wind and rain's blown;—
I've done my best to hang on, as they tried to whittle
the name from the action, the flesh away from the bone,

but I think, sometimes, I'm fighting a losing battle.
So many bad nights; so many strange homes to burgle,
and every job done with a mate I don't know :—
oh, you're all right; I don't mean to be personal,
but when the day breaks, you'll have your orders, and go.

Then, the next time the foul weather howls in the ginnel;
when the slates slide, the brimming gutters gurgle;
there'll be another lad I've never seen before,
with the rest of the knowledge that makes the job possible
as I ease up a window or skeleton-key a door.

Still, it's my only life, and I've no quarrel
with the boss's methods;—apart from the odd quibble
about allowances and fair rates of pay,
or the difficult routes I often have to travel,
or the fact that I never get a holiday.

Most of the time, though, I'm glad of mere survival,
even at the stormiest hour of the darkest vigil.
. . . Here's the hall door; under the stairs, you said?
This one's easy, because the old folk are feeble,
and lie in their curtained room, sleeping like the dead.

Sometimes, believe me, it's a lot more trouble,
when you've got to be silent, and move as though through treacle.
Now hold your breath while I let these tumblers click . . .
I've done these many a time . . . a well known model;
one more turn now . . . Yes; that does the trick.

Nothing inside? The same recurrent muddle;
I think the most careful plan's a bloody marvel
if it plays you true, if nothing at all goes wrong.
Well, let's be off; we've another place to tackle
under the blown, black, rain; and the dawn won't be long

when the wind will drop, and the rain become a drizzle,
and you'll go your way. Leaving me the bedraggled
remnants of night, that walk within the head
long after the sun-shot gutters cease to trickle,
and I draw my curtains, and topple into bed.

*

ST. MARK'S, CHEETHAM HILL

DESIGNED to dominate the district—
God being nothing if not large
and stern, melancholic from man's fall
(like Victoria widowed early)—
the church, its yard, were raised on a plateau
six feet above the surrounding green.
There weren't many houses then; Manchester
was a good walk away. I've seen
faded photographs: the church standing
amidst strolling gentry, as though
ready to sail for the Empire's farthest parts;—
the union jack at the tower's masthead
enough to quell upstart foreigners and natives.
But those were the early days. The city
began to gollop profits, burst
outward on all sides. Soon,
miles of the cheapest brick swaddled landmarks,
the church one. Chimes that had used to wake
workers in Whitefield, died in near streets.

44

From our house—a part of the parish—
St. Mark's is a turn right, a turn left,
and straight down Coke Street past the *Horseshoe*.
The raised graveyard—full these many years—
overlooks the junction of five streets;
pollarded plane trees round its edge,
the railings gone to help fight Hitler.
Adam Murray of New Galloway,
'Who much improved the spinning mule',
needs but a step from his tomb to peer in
at somebody's glittering television;
Harriet Pratt, 'A native of Derby',
might sate her judgement-hunger with chips
were she to rise and walk twenty yards.
The houses are that close. The church,
begrimed, an ugly irregular box
squatting above those who once filled it
with faith and praise, looks smaller now
than in those old pictures. Subdued
by a raincoat factory's bulk, the Kosher
Slaughter House next door, its dignity
is rare weddings, the Co-op hearse,
and hired cars full of elderly mourners.

The congregations are tiny these days;
few folk could tell you whether it's 'High' or 'Low';
the vicar's name, the times of services,
is specialized knowledge. And fear has gone;
the damp, psalmed, God of my childhood has gone.
Perhaps a boy delivering papers
in winter darkness before the birds wake,
keeps to Chapel Street's far side, for fear
some corpse interred at his ankle's depth
might shove a hand through the crumbling wall
and grab him in passing; but not for fear
of black religion—the blurred bulk
of God in drizzle and dirty mist,

45

or hooded with snow on his white throne
watching the sparrow fall.

               Now, the graveyard,
its elegant wrought-ironwork wrenched,
carted away; its rhymed epitaphs,
urns of stone and ingenious scrolls,
chipped, tumbled, masked by weeds,
is used as a playground. Shouting children
Tiggy between the tombs.

               On Saturdays
I walk there sometimes—through the drift
of jazz from open doors, the tide
of frying fish, and the groups of women
gossiping on their brushes—to see the church,
its God decamped, or dead, or daft
to all but the shrill hosannas of children
whose prayers are laughter, playing such parts
in rowdy games, you'd think it built
for no greater purpose, think its past
one long term of imprisonment.

There's little survives Authority's cant
that's not forgotten, written-off,
or misunderstood. The Methodist Chapel's
been bought by the Jews for a Synagogue;
Ukrainian Catholics have the Wesleyan's
sturdy structure built to outlast Rome—
which clings to its holy snowball down the street;
and men of the district say St. Mark's
is part of a clearance area. Soon
it will be down as low as rubble
from every house that squeezed it round,
to bed a motorway and a new estate.
Or worse : repainted, pointed, primmed—
as becomes a unit in town-planners'
clever dreams of a healthy community—
will prosper in dignity and difference,
the gardened centre of new horizons.

Rather than this, I'd see it smashed,
and picture the final splendours of decay:
Opposing gangs in wild 'Relievo',
rushing down aisles and dusty pews
at which the houses look straight in
past broken wall; and late-night drunkards
stumbling their usual short-cut home
across uneven eulogies, fumbling
difficult flies to pour discomfort out
in comfortable shadows, in a nave
they praise with founts, and moonlit blooms of steam.

*

INVASION OF THE HOUSE

THIN in the ear as a bat's squeak,
　　and through the house all night like bats swarming,
　　dodging and darting from room to room—
a piped pattern upon the dark hours—
　　is the laughter, the moan, the disturbed talk
of all the household gods. The flowers

loll on the landing. From her bed
　　the mother of many men (seventy years—
　　and thirty of them widowed—bleared
to whistling breath and no voice) raises
　　a hand in the face of the crowding dead,
summoning sons that have never known her praise

to lean to her mouth from the world's end
　　that, if there's strength enough, she may revile
　　each and every one: the cruel
issue of love. Young stay-at-home awakes
　　suddenly at the pushed sheets' small sound;
chair-cramp forgotten, his headache

in someone else's skull where shrill
   laughter and howls of grief and busy chatter
   swoop from the rafters' gloom, then scatter.
His mother lies, fists clenched, face set
   to a fierce stare, as if in death her will
survived, like the growth of grey beneath her hair-net.

Kingdoms away, in the next room,
   awkwardly swagged and heavy with chirruping dreams,
   his young wife sleeps, her moist palms
against her belly's hump, wherein there stirs
   the son eager to quit the womb,
and get at her breasts, and share this house of hers.

*

BANK HOLIDAY

BRIGHT eyes in a pile of lumber
watching the spanking miles unroll
a seaside day in easy summer
   enter running or not at all
to the bodies without number
whoop of children swoop of gulls
   A lively tune on a tin whistle.

Blazing noon on a metal tangle
see the fat lady's skeleton mate,
Come and Get It, I'm No Angel,
   Kiss Me Quick Before It's Too Late;
Oh the bright and battering sandal
on the concrete's waste of heat
   Enter running or not at all.

Sandy mythologies by the mister
dribble nose and fly blown loose,
flags' and hands' heroic gestures;
   an old hat filling with booze

while the roaring roller coaster
flees its maze above the nudes
    Kiss me quick before it's too late.

Candy floss sticks, syrup waffles,
secret rides in the River Caves,
Scenes of the Harem, Sights Unlawful;
    widows and hucksters thick as thieves
and the day tilts at the bottle
and the starstruck girls believe.
    An old hat filling with booze.

Take me an air trip round the Tower
where, all glorious within,
spangles of the dancing floor
    shake a big bellyful of din
and balloons in splendid shower
fall to zips and hearts undone
    Widows and hucksters thick as thieves.

Rotherham Stockport Salford Nelson
Sheffield Burnley Bradford Shaw
roll by a shining Cinderella
    into the night's enormous maw,
smashin girl and luvly fella
tip the wink and close the door.
    Shake a big bellyful of din.

Sodden straws and french letters,
trodden ices, orange hulls,
clotted beach and crowded gutters.
    A lively tune on a tin whistle
sings to the sea 'What matters . . . matters'
and the street sweepers and the gulls,
    Into the night's enormous maw.

*

49

In Autumn, begin.
                    Uprooting geraniums,
shaking them gently for storage in darkness,
had heard guns crackle in far streets.
In the deepening sky, one evening,
an airman wrote 'Love'—a vaporous trail
gone before sunset.
                   Beyond the city, mountains;
most often hidden. On clear days, certain fields,
a pike, glinting glass. Many went that way,
wheels rumbling towards rock.
                         None saw a good end.
The last birds flew late. South, eagerly
when they went; still, sparrows at my door
importuned for what bread?

   Guard against draughts; bolt the banging door.

Sat late by small oil, a moth, and one moment's silence.
Books helped me, so did other things:
crossword puzzles; meditation.
                     November rain
stained the chimney breast;
at night the wounded groaned beyond the hedge.
The sink froze.
               All day long the tanks clattered past,
disturbing earth, churning up cobbles;
not a face I knew; guns pointing onward.

   Christmas is nothing without a child.

Ghosts again in the front room.
I thought they'd gone for good, but meaning no harm.
Seeking their own echoes, I think;
their faces in mirrors.
                 And then. . . .
New men with the first green shoots;

declarations; manifestoes; promises
in shoddy eccentric type on grey paper.
'There will be public trials . . .

                              full restitution . . .'
Dreamed often : four friends dead;
one in exile; one a traitor to some cause;
but could not say the rest.
After the big winds the battle came back;

                              muddled,
beyond the understanding of many.
The snipers stayed longest,

                    and the sky brightened,
imperceptibly, towards summer.
Twigs from laburnum cluttered the front path;
one branch snapped abruptly while I watched,
suggesting more death.

  Sharpen the good saw.

Noticed willowherb in unlikely places :
on the roofs of lavatories; in formal gardens.
Dock leaf and dandelion brightened the ruins
beyond my care.

                    The cat went out; never came back,
but the strawberries ripened well; this gave pleasure.
In the topmost room, the lodger, enfeebled,
scrabbled the quilt, called for a priest,

                              or rabbi.
Only a lay preacher came, and he starved and rambling.

  Trim the hedge; sweep the cellar; send letters.

One day it was over, or seemed to be;

                         someone said
a van with a loudspeaker telling good news . . .
I think someone said that; and near the end
the birds came back; or perhaps they just came out
to see August with the din of brass-bands,

flaunting banners, throwing down arms in the street.
How the children shouted!

How the women cried!
I smiled in the garden, clutching a dead root,
and the thrush stood on the aerial opposite,
singing! singing!

Old friends returned;
drank my new wine;

I welcomed them home.

*

AT A HOTEL

PERHAPS that was the most
appropriate place of all,
for only late-coming drunkards
prowled in the deserted passages,
where the living cared least, and the dead
could not be expected to call,
pouring in the midnight ear
their usual muddling messages.
What they had gone there for
that night neither of them knew,
though both devised ritual
music to name the occasion.
When he came to her room she thought
it important that the carpet was blue,
while he saw clearly their naked
nearness, and summoned up passion.
Knowing little of love,
much less of innocence,
they lay in a dark heat
without ecstasy or shame,
both bowing and scraping
in a palace of self-pretence,

whose king had no face, and whose
courtiers were blind and lame—
she at a ceremony,
he too in a crowded hall
where drunken revellers exchanged
intimate, incoherent, messages:

outside the uninvited,
who could not be expected to call,
waited, dumbly waited,
in the ill-lit deserted passages.

*

OCTOBER IN CLOWES PARK

THE day dispossessed of light. At four o'clock
in the afternoon, a sulphurous, manufactured
twilight, smudging the scummed lake's far side,
leant on the park. Sounds, muffled—
as if the lolling muck clogged them at the source—
crawled to the ear. A skyed ball thudded
to ground, a swan leathered its wings by the island.
I stood and watched a water-hen arrow
shutting silver across the sooty mat
of the lake's surface, an earl's lake,
though these fifty years the corporation's,
and what is left of the extensive estate—
a few acres of scruffy, flat land
framing this wet sore in the minds of property agents—
a public park. All else is built on.
Through swags of trees poked the bare backsides
of encircling villas, garages, gardening-sheds,
a ring of lights making the park dimmer.
Boys and men shouldering long rods—
all licensed fishers, by their open way—
scuffled the cinders past me, heading for home,

but I stayed on; the dispossessed day
held me, turned me towards the ruined Hall.
Pulsing in that yellow, luminous, murk
(a trick of the eye), the bits of broken pillar
built into banks, the last upright wall,
the stalactite-hung split shells of stables,
seemed likely to find a voice—such pent-in grief
and anger!—or perhaps to explode silently
with force greater than any known to progress,
wiping the district, town, kingdom, age,
to darkness far deeper than that which fluffed
now at the neat new urinal's outline,
and heaved and beat behind it in the ruins.
Like a thud in the head, suddenly become memory,
stillness was dumb around me. Scrambling up
a heap of refuse, I grabbed at crystalled brick.
Flakes fell from my hand—a gruff tinkle—
no knowledge there of what brought the Hall low,
or concern either. Neither did I care.
Irrecoverably dead, slumped in rank weed
and billowy grass, it mouldered from here to now,
connoting nothing but where my anger stood
and grief enough to pull the sagging smoke
down from the sky, a silent, lethal, swaddling
over the garden I played in as a child,
and over those children—laughter in the branches—
shaking the pear-tree's last sour fruit to ground.

*

THE LOOK OF LOVE

BELEAGUERED by passions, as by thunder
of encircling arms, some ate dirt,
became louse-ridden, waxed holy
by degrees of deprivation
and fits of weakness; withstood the hordes,
entertained not their grinning Gods,
and died virgins, at length, slowly.

Some explored a metaphor
nearer to home. Local affections,
pursued through fog, a maze of streets,
finally left them, dazed and tricked,
writing, in lieu of love poems,
a pocket guide to their own district.

Saints and fools. Some, who were neither,
(like you and I) bit lips in kisses,
groaned beneath weight of thrusting flesh,
or tried to deal gently with another.
To these the scale of things was plain;
but *they* surrendered, gathered fat
like foreign honours, or went out
to the corner shop and were never seen again.

*

AN EMPTY HOUSE

Doors bolted; windows dirt-bleared.
Was ever invitation sent
to cross this garden, vilely littered
with ashes, garbage, once-elegant

columned Olympians;—toppled, broken?
No; but rabid ignoramus,
feckless far-from-home, wise man
exceeding wisdom, and various

frustrated ghosts, hover, strut,
slouch, and scribble in these grounds.
Forgotten squatters, from mere habit
raising occasional, imploring, hands

in antic faith. A common blindness
fudges with wishes dead hope;
the towers are fallen that were topless;
nothing left but strife, wrought shape!

Some few, compelled by pride to seek
the truth, scream, curse, take poison,
weep until their hearts break,
peering on cobwebs, splendour gone.

The best, sad-eyed, quick with courage,
admit an ending. Gather, dustbin
their old love-letters, damp from the garage,
and leave to work, to father children.

*

MRS. ROOT

BUSYBODY, nosey-parker
lacking the vast discretion of most
was this woman. The self-cast
chief mourner at funerals, worker
at weddings, she could sniff out death
in a doctor's optimism, joggle
a maiden's mind (button-holed on the front path)
till virginity bit like filed teeth.

Prepared, without discrimination,
friend and enemy for the grave.
Washed, talcumed them all. A woman
who wore such ceremonies like a glove,
could console a grief-struck household
that hardly knew her name, and then
collect money for a wreath fit to wield
at a Queen's passing. Death-skilled

but no less wedding-wise,
her hand stitched the perfecting dart
in bridal satin; she brought report
of cars arriving, clear skies
towards the church. They were her tears
(pew-stifled) from which the happiest
laughter billowed confetti outside the black doors.
Of best wishes, loudest were hers.

And nobody thanked her; Why doesn't
she mind her own business?, they said
who'd leant upon her. Crude and peasant-like
her interest in brides, and the dead.
I thought so too, yet still was loath
to add my voice, sensing that
my secret poems were like her actions: both
pried into love and savoured death.

*

NOVEMBER NIGHT

THE fire roars in the boiler-back,
   pots and pans in neat rows
   swell in the lamplight's friendly shadows,
tomorrow's shirt hangs from the rack.

Trails at my ear a turned-back cuff,
   as though in assurance, this shirt:
   yesterday's stains, yesterday's dirt,
unknown to such starched, immaculate stuff.

A gilded hand grasps paid-up bills
   prettily, on a gleaming hook,
   in the cupboard a fragrant cake
waits to be cut, the kettle boils.

The house murmurs; its peace abounds
   with suave civilities. I have heard
   much quiet insistence : 'All is mastered :
beds have been warmed, the clocks wound,

dead men tucked tight in earth,
   their errors with them; rest your head,
   for, see—all is cared-for, tidied.'
Nodding a Yes not come to mouth,

yet must I prowl from room to room,
   upstairs and down, in dark corners
   where damp exudes, cellar-brick furs,
and old dust piles in the rafter's gloom;

and must I heave these curtains wide
   upon fog, like a blind wall
   hemming the house. Neither voice nor footfall
sounds from the nothingness outside,

nor is there warmth of blanket's load
   can pinion my sleep tonight from cold
   nightmares of flight through windows sealed
against the encasing death of God.

*

From FOR A LOST GIRL
IV

IF you would have it sole criterion—
   the upthrust in your belly—let me go;
eyes roll white for some other, stay
   at finishing school for ever when I'm gone.

But know, this biter of your breasts, lord
   of your loins, grew from such a loud stock,
that was no sensuous essay, no sex-trick,
   but what generations in his ears roared

of love and death. You will not find its match
   in any bed where love's a lesser pain,
or where you're worshipped, or where simpler men
   importune you with love that's pure, not hotch-potch.

Seek (if ever sickened by girlhood's ease
   of animal joy, and answers that come pat)
a man who, like me, trails his fool's coat
   only to hood his thought; whose eyes, from yours,

turn blankly, at odd times, towards rooms
   you cannot visit. His thrust with fire and flood
enough to raze your proud state will be powered,
   and if he leaves your arms to write poems,

or raise his family dead, be glad that he
   is troubled so, for to your bed he'll bring
creation's endless comedy in the strong
   heave of his arse, his longing to be free.

*

VII

PORTO VENERE

ONE midnight, glittering-eyed, in restless silence,
she left our bed, the tower where we were lodged,
and hurried to the sea. The moon was full.
Over the lanterns in the square, the dancing
couples who'd stay till dawn, it swung seaward
through legions of tiny clouds; and she—high-breasted
beside the harbour's fidget of clunking boats—
blanched and burrowed among the shifting shadows,
hearing only the lonely grotto's roar—
like the moon's voice, or the voice of her own blood.

I did not see her go, but dozed heavy
with wine under the wounds of a pallid icon,
and dreamed her body clung so close to mine
sprindrift of sweat scattered from huge surges
of muscled battering, undertow sucked back
surfacing faces, thrust, and filled, and killed
everything but the sea's; until she lay
salty and heavy-eyed within my arms,
murmuring : 'Love, the waves, the waves were awful.
The moon went in. I thought that I might drown.'

*

X

You—whose own flesh is your despair,
whose heart's grown-up enough to hate
its vagaries, but not to control them,
whose love—escaped its one strong leash—
rampages here, there, everywhere,

crying itself to sleep in beds
you have no knowledge of, or hope—
be quiet for me; learn stillness.
Not claiming more than any man
(being the brute force, and Gods

foolish and fond, which make you such
a torment to yourself), is wise
to claim; but poet, clown, and lover—
for his troubles far from your bed—
I pen these wooden words as crutch

under your weakness, thumb my nose,
tumble and joke, to point the wit
of self-known human silly kind,
and will not shed a single tear
for fear you'll strike the tragic pose

XI

of raving to ruin. Dear, all lips
are much the same in darkness, mine
no different, perhaps, for being mine,
but I have eyes to recommend me,
keen to your smallest mole, and hopes

you'll mystify always, since I am
he who is gifted with you whole.
Be still. No novelties suffice
where custom, truth, and puzzlement
cleave together to make a home.

*

My Love who last night, the destroyer
    of ordered settlements, swung her breasts
to crash down trees, and sturdily housed
    communities trod to the ground beneath her flat-footed power,

this morning, Queen among her people,
    weeps for the homeless, visits death
and succours the dying—grim with grief
    that God has seen fit to visit her reign with such trouble.

*

XII

I love you as I love the world,
    turning away often to retch
bile and bits I cannot hold

in guts grown gross on the rich
    diet of thirty years. Goddess—
naked or clothed—wife, bitch,

woman forever anonymous,
   known only by your open thighs
moist beneath mine in pitch darkness,

will you be content with lies—
   darling, my dear darling sweetheart—
that I should love you less than this

grave-ridden place in which I'm set—
   down, amid stinking histories,
with all the wombs of earth to brat?

*

CHILD'S BOUNCING SONG

MOLLY VICKERS
wets her knickers,
Georgie's father's big and black,
cream on Sunday
milk on Monday,
I'm the cock of all the back.

Tell me whose a
bigger boozer
Mister Baker beats them all,
from his lorry
watch him hurry,
touch the ground and touch the wall.

Who're the gentry
down our entry—
Mrs. Smith's got two T.V.'s.
What if her coat
is a fur coat,
all her kids are full of fleas.

Joan loves Harry,
Jack will marry
Edna when they both grow up,
I'll announce it,
bounce bounce bounce it,
our dog Whiskers' had a pup.

High and low and
to and fro and
down the street and up the hill,
Mrs. Cuthbert's
husband snuffed it,
she got nothing from his will.

Mister, mister,
Shirley's sister
won a prize on Blackpool prom,
mam'll smother
our kid brother
when the school inspectors come.

Skip and hopping
I'm off shopping,
Tuesday night it's pie for tea,
please to take this
ball and make this
song of bouncing song for me.

A WOMAN DYING

In a room with a wardrobe far too large—
bought at a sale cheap, or handed down—
this careless woman struggled for breath.
Faded oilcloth stopped short of the skirting boards;
beneath her pyjama-top there flowered
the vivid, cancerous sores. She lay with death.

Chrysanthemums in a white bowl
held their tongues, were not telling the name
of whoever had brought them. Now and then
neighbours and friends appeared to be by her side.
Her husband came, spoke, went,—so did the pain;
nightdark, daylight, nightdark, and daylight again.

Already nothingness hung like a smell
among the factual furniture. The bare
bulb in its rusty socket rocked
substance away as her younger sister slept.
'Is that burglars?' she said in the small hours,
who had never worried whether the door was locked.

Something was different; something had come in
through fifty-six years of doors left on the latch,
that fed on neglected duties: dust
gathering unswept, meals she'd forgotten to make.
Perhaps it would go if she did her best:
on tiny observances she fretted dully and fussed.

But could not make redress, nor pay
attention enough to keep her sister's face
sharp as her memory of it. Trees
beyond the window waved branches of good-bye,
and then: 'What was it the branches waved?'
Question and answer were like as two peas.

And neither mattered. The pain blanked out
everything but a lusting after death,
or youth, or sleep—they looked the same.
Whatever knew friendly flesh was good, was God.
She choked and spat and coughed and tore
down Heaven with moans until the doctor came.

A needle eased the world away.
She did not see the window's curdled shine
grow fronds and flowers which multiplied
all night despite that thrusting, fiery, breath.
At dawn winter went on without her,
while by the bed her sister stood and cried.

*

AN EVENING AT HOME

Sensing a poem about to happen,
two letters demanded to be written.

One to a man about a dog
began clearly and ended vaguely;

the other, to a girl for old times' sake,
overstepped the bounds of propriety. My teeth began to ache.

From a single suspect raw-edged tooth
the pain spread all over my mouth

before I could stop it. Coupled with
rising flatulence, it nearly overcame faith

in my sacred calling. But back I fought
with a concentration of poetic thought

upon my desk. I almost went over
from the chair in which I'd sat to recover—

and would have done had not the lodger knocked
to say that his sink waste-pipe was blocked.

Using the plunger, I began to feel jaded
and disillusioned; something more was needed

than mere poems to right the world.
My hands were numb; I remembered the millions killed

in God's name; I remembered bombs, gas-chambers, famine,
    poverty,
and my greying hair. I could not write poetry.

My nose tingled as though it was going to bleed;
I shut my notebook quietly and went to bed.

*

METAMORPHOSES OF THE VAMPIRE

After Baudelaire

THE mouth I longed for, like a heavy fruit
split in its over-ripeness, gaped above me,
breasts tipped by horny nipples rasped my chest,
and 'Love' I cried, 'Oh Love', while in that cavern
deep in her flesh she sucked my life away
with merciless flexings, and the fruit swung down
oilily dripping words like scented juices:
'Die further inside me, die my happy man,—
no need for conscience, I am first and last.
Salvation's in my breasts, grasp at it, bite them;
God's in my womb, thrust upwards to his light,
I'm planets, constellations, galaxies,
I'm birth, and death, and love, and day and night.'

The fruit's wet pith engulfed me. In a dream
I staggered the crazy beds of endless rivers,
thirsting to screams beneath a black sun,
and toppling, died amidst my empty veins.

I woke craving the fruit; turning to kiss her
my parched lips met a lolling sack of blood
shaped like a giant doll. I fell back
through drums of spinning blackness, till the dawn
opened my eyes to the heap of dry bones
assembling by my side : a skeleton
that squawked three times inanely, and was gone.

*

MY FATHER'S WALKING-STICK

SWINDLER, con-man, and embezzler,
are a few of the roles my father played.
Declared a bankrupt in '32,
he opened a radio shop in my mother's name,
forging her signature to save time and trouble.
She was the only daughter among
a pack of lads—the last at home,
when he met her. She and a widowed mother
in a well-kept house. No wonder his lodger's eye
brightened towards the ageing girl.
Soon my grandma was baking him meat pies,
calling him 'Son'.

               It must have seemed
a good arrangement to all concerned : he—
with the urge to procreate that visits
philandering men after years of contraceptives,
but no home-making instinct—found
a home already made; my mother,
fiercely dutiful, thought she could add
a husband to what existed; my grandma
imagined daughter and self provided for.
Perhaps there was love, too. I can't
answer for that, although my mother,
even at sixty-nine's a sucker for silver-tongued men.

67

Snapshots show him in a cap
with a big neb, his arm round her
on a boat to the Isle of Man; both
are smiling, three months before my birth.
Later, there's one of her in a laughing pose
next to the backyard dustbin. Taken
by him, it looks affectionate—as though
he'd said, as he clicked the shutter : 'Let's
have it backwards-road-about tonight.'
But my mother's fervent, legal, honesty
must have shocked him. Out of bed
he couldn't persuade her to accept
his improvisations. When angry creditors
and detectives called, she jibbed at saying :
'I'm sorry, he's gone to London on business.'
According to their different lights
they let each other down badly. I was five
when he disappeared with a Royal Warrant
out for his arrest. None of us saw
him again, but twenty years on,
incredibly breaking silence, came news
of his distant death.
                                   Among his belongings
(the woman he'd lived with had them in a cardboard
grocery box, ready for me to claim or reject)
I found a stout walking-stick.
Thinking it apt that, having been
without support from him for so long,
my mother should have something of him
to lean on at last, I carried it home
three hundred miles under my arm.

Her comment was flat, but had an edge
I couldn't name :
                              'Put it in the hall-stand.'
There it has stood, unused, to this day.

*

FASHIONABLE POET READING

He has forgone the razor for a year
to hide from himself his mooning eunuch's smile.
His eye—a disease devouring detail—
finds poems in everything. Should he fail
to feed silence to death, he might think himself queer.

Page after page his active verbs perform
their masculine tricks, his syntax bares muscles
in a fighting stance through which the poor blood thrills
a wishful dream of health. He wills
significant scale on nothings, lest his infirm

grasp of the world appal him, and his claim
to deserved fame be openly suspect. Doubt
must still be howled down : sweating, he bellows out
his repertoire. Fat and guilt
begin to dissolve. He shouts. He is glad he came.

*

HILL-TOP AND GUY FAWKES

Not more than his nose and one eye
was showing. He lurked, as though shy
of being caught looking—like an elderly spinster
behind her curtains when a wedding goes by.

Before we saw him seemed like an age
of fishing become shove and nudge;
one of the boys shouted, and there he was poking
slyly dead through the looped-back scum on the lodge.

The police came with iron hooks.
They shooed us off. We made tracks
behind the rusting dump of machinery
and, still as cogs among the little hillocks

of clinker, watched while they dragged him out.
The newspaper said he was seventy-eight,
'Of no fixed abode', we played at being vagrants
the rest of the summer holidays, hobbling about

with sacking on our feet, and caps
held out for pennies. Then the shops
began to sell fireworks, and in our fathers' cellars
we laboured to build the burnable human shapes.

In the north of England a lodge is a small reservoir beside a mill.

*

THE POET'S AGE

IT visits you at night. You have awakened
from damp, barbarous dreams to this worse thing
haunting the house in which your family sleeps.

You cannot see, or hear, or feel it, although
the black becoming lumpy with your possessions,
the small sigh from the cot, even your wife's

delicate flank against your rough flesh,
are terrible in its presence. You will not rise
to seek assurance from your poems. Lying

breathless with fear you know they were not worth it.
You will not rise to smile upon your son;
he is growing towards your death. You will not turn

to find companionship; you had young loves,
but that was long ago. You sweat in a staring
silence through which the rolling planet speeds,

you and that thing you jollify with birthdays,
dignify with position, charm, and honours,
you and this lustful, ravening, killing thing.

*

*

CHARLES TOMLINSON

*

REALITY is to be sought, not in concrete,
But in space made articulate:
The shore, for instance,
Spreading between wall and wall,
The sea-voice
Tearing the silence from the silence.

*

FLUTE MUSIC

THERE is a moment for speech and for silence.
Lost between possibilities
But deploring a forced harmony,
We elect the flute.

A season, defying gloss, may be the sum
Of blue water beneath green rain;
It may comprise comets, days, lakes
Yet still bear the exegesis of music.

Seeing and speaking we are two men:
The eye encloses as a window—a flute
Governs the land, its winter and its silence.

The flute is uncircumscribed by moonlight or irised mornings.
It moves with equal certainty
Through a register of palm-greens and flesh-rose.

The glare of brass over a restless bass
(Red glow across olive twilight)
Urges to a delighted excess,
A weeping among broken gods.

The flute speaks (reason's song
Riding the ungovernable wave)
The bound of passion
Out of the equitable core of peace.

*

THROUGH BINOCULARS

In their congealed light
We discover that what we had taken for a face
Has neither eyes nor mouth,
But only the impersonality of anatomy.

Silencing movement,
They withdraw life.

Definition grows clear-cut, but bodiless,
Withering by a dimension.

To see thus
Is to ignore the revenge of light on shadow,
To confound both in a brittle and false union.

This fictive extension into madness
Has a kind of bracing effect:
That normality is, after all, desirable
One can no longer doubt having experienced its opposite.

Binoculars are the last phase in a romanticism:
The starkly mad vision, not mortal,
But dangling one in a vicarious, momentary idiocy.

To dispense with them
Is to make audible the steady roar of evening,
Withdrawing in slow ripples of orange,
Like the retreat of water from sea-caves.

*

FIASCHERINO

Over an ash-fawn beach fronting a sea which keeps
    Rolling and unrolling, lifting
The green fringes from submerged rocks
    On its way in, and, on its way out
Dropping them again, the light

Squanders itself, a saffron morning
   Advances among foam and stones, sticks
Clotted with black naphtha
   And frayed to the newly carved
Fresh white of chicken flesh.

One leans from the cliff-top. Height
   Distances like an inverted glass; the shore
Is diminished but concentrated, jewelled
   With the clarity of warm colours
That, seen more nearly, would dissipate

Into masses. This map-like interplay
   Of sea-light against shadow
And the mottled close-up of wet rocks
   Drying themselves in the hot air
Are lost to us. Content with our portion,

Where, we ask ourselves, is the end of all this
   Variety that follows us? Glare
Pierces muslin; its broken rays
   Hovering in trembling filaments
Glance on the ceiling with no more substance

Than a bee's wing. Thickening, these
   Hang down over the pink walls
In green bars, and, flickering between them,
   A moving fan of two colours,
The sea unrolls and rolls itself into the low room.

*

THE ATLANTIC

Launched into an opposing wind, hangs
   Grappled beneath the onrush,
And there, lifts, curling in spume,
   Unlocks, drops from that hold
Over and shoreward. The beach receives it,
   A whitening line, collapsing

Powdering-off down its broken length;
  Then, curded, shallow, heavy
With clustering bubbles, it nears
  In a slow sheet that must climb
Relinquishing its power, upward
  Across tilted sand. Unravelled now
And the shore, under its lucid pane,
  Clear to the sight, it is spent:
The sun rocks there, as the netted ripple
  Into whose skeins the motion threads it
Glances athwart a bed, honey-combed
  By heaving stones. Neither survives the instant
But is caught back, and leaves, like the after-image
  Released from the floor of a now different mind,
A quick gold, dyeing the uncovering beach
  With sunglaze. That which we were,
Confronted by all that we are not,
  Grasps in subservience its replenishment.

*

TRAMONTANA AT LERICI

TODAY, should you let fall a glass, it would
  Disintegrate, played off with such keenness
Against the cold's resonance (the sounds
  Hard, separate and distinct, dropping away
In a diminishing cadence) that you might swear
  This was the imitation of glass falling.

Leaf-dapples sharpen. Emboldened by this clarity
  The minds of artificers would turn prismatic
Running on lace perforated in crisp wafers
  That could cut like steel. Constitutions,
Drafted under this fecund chill would be annulled
  For the strictness of their equity, the moderation of their pity.

At evening, one is alarmed by such definition
    In as many lost greens as one will give glances to recover,
As many again which the landscape
    Absorbing into the steady dusk, condenses
From aquamarine to that slow indigo-pitch
    Where the light and twilight abandon themselves.

And the chill grows. In this air
    Unfit for politicians and romantics
Dark hardens from blue, effacing the windows:
    A tangible block, it will be no accessory
To that which does not concern it. One is ignored
    By so much cold suspended in so much night.

*

NORTHERN SPRING

Nor is this the setting for extravagance. Trees
    Fight with the wind, the wind eludes them
Streaking its cross-lanes over the uneasy water
    Whose bronze whitens. To emulate such confusion
One must impoverish the resources of folly,
    But to taste it is medicinal. Consider

How through that broken calm, as the sun emerges,
    The sky flushes its blue, dyeing the grass
In the promise of a more stable tone:
    Less swift however than the cloud is wide—
Its shadow (already) quenching the verdure
    As its bulk muffles the sun—the blue drains
And the assault renews in colourless ripples.

Then, lit, the scene deepens. Where should one look
    In the profusion of possibilities? One conceives
Placing before them a square house
    Washed in the coolness of lime, a hub
For the scattered deployment, to define
    In pure white from its verdant ground
The variegated excess which threatens it.

77

Spring lours. Neither will the summer achieve
   That Roman season of an equable province
Where the sun is its own witness and the shadow
   Measures its ardour with the impartiality
Of the just. Evening, debauching this sky, asks
   To be appraised and to be withstood.

*

PARING THE APPLE

THERE are portraits and still-lives.

And there is paring the apple.

And then? Paring it slowly,
From under cool-yellow
Cold-white emerging. And ... ?

The spring of concentric peel
Unwinding off white,
The blade hidden, dividing.

There are portraits and still-lives
And the first, because 'human'
Does not excel the second, and
Neither is less weighted
With a human gesture, than paring the apple
With a human stillness.

The cool blade
Severs between coolness, apple-rind
Compelling a recognition.

*

MORE FOREIGN CITIES

'Nobody wants any more poems about foreign cities . . .'
(From a recent disquisition on poetics.)

NOT forgetting Ko-jen, that
Musical city (it has
Few buildings, and annexes
Space by combating silence),
There is Fiordiligi, its sun-changes
Against walls of transparent stone
Unsettling all preconception—a city
For architects (they are taught
By casting their nets
Into those moving shoals); and there is
Kairouan, whose lit space
So slides into and fits
The stone masses, one would doubt
Which was the more solid
Unless, folding back
Gold segments out of the white
Pith globe of a quartered orange,
One may learn perhaps
To read such perspectives. At Luna
There is a city of bridges, where
Even the inhabitants are mindful
Of a shared privilege: a bridge
Does not exist for its own sake.
It commands vacancy.

*

CÉZANNE AT AIX

AND the mountain: each day
Immobile like fruit. Unlike, also
—Because irreducible, because
Neither a component of the delicious

And therefore questionable,
Nor distracted (as the sitter)
By his own pose and, therefore,
Doubly to be questioned : it is not
Posed. It is. Untaught
Unalterable, a stone bridgehead
To that which is tangible
Because unfelt before. There
In its weathered weight
Its silence silences, a presence
Which does not present itself.

*

FAREWELL TO VAN GOGH

THE quiet deepens. You will not persuade
    One leaf of the accomplished, steady, darkening
Chestnut-tower to displace itself
    With more of violence than the air supplies
When, gathering dusk, the pond brims evenly
    And we must be content with stillness.

Unhastening, daylight withdraws from us its shapes
    Into their central calm. Stone by stone
Your rhetoric is dispersed until the earth
    Becomes once more the earth, the leaves
A sharp partition against cooling blue.

Farewell, and for your instructive frenzy
    Gratitude. The world does not end tonight
And the fruit that we shall pick tomorrow
    Await us, weighing the unstripped bough.

*

WALKING by map, I chose unwonted ground,
  A crooked, questionable path which led
Beyond the margin, then delivered me
  At a turn. Red marl
Had rutted the aimless track
  That firmly withheld the recompense it hid
Till now, close by its end, the day's discoveries
  Began with the dimming night.

A house. The wall-stones, brown.
  The doubtful light, more of a mist than light
Floating at hedge-height through the sodden fields
  Had yielded, or a final glare
Burst there, rather, to concentrate
  Sharp saffron, as the ebbing year—
Or so it seemed, for the dye deepened—poured
  All of its yellow strength through the way I went:

Over grass, garden-space, over the grange
  That jutted beyond, lengthening-down
The house line, tall as it was,
  By tying it to the earth, trying its pride
(Which submitted) under a nest of barns,
  A walled weight of lesser encumbrances—
Few of which worsened it, and none
  As the iron sheds, sealing my own approach.

All stone. I had passed these last, unwarrantable
  Symbols of—no;—let me define, rather
The thing they were not, all that we cannot be,
  By the description, simply of that which merits it:
Stone. Why must (as it does at each turn)
  Each day, the mean rob us of patience, distract us
Before even its opposite—before stone, which
  Cut, piled, mortared, is patience's presence.

The land farmed, the house was neglected: but
 Gashed panes (and there were many) still showed
Into the pride of that presence. I had reached
 Unchallenged, within feet of the door
Ill-painted, but at no distant date—the least
 Our prodigal time could grudge it; paused
To measure the love, to assess its object,
 That trusts for continuance to the mason's hand.

Five centuries—here were (at the least) five—
 In linked love, eager excrescence
Where the door, arched, crowned with acanthus,
 Aimed at a civil elegance, but hit
This sturdier compromise, neither Greek, Gothic
 Nor Strawberry, clumped from the arching-point
And swatheing down, like a fist of wheat,
 The unconscious emblem for the house's worth.

Conclusion surrounded it, and the accumulation
 After Lammas-growth. Still coming on
Heart's-tongue by maiden-hair
 Thickened beneath the hedges, the corn levelled
And carried, long-since; but the earth
 (Its tint glowed in the house wall)
Out of the reddish dark still thrust up foison
 Through the browning-back of the exhausted year:

Thrust through the unweeded yard, where earth and house
 Debated the terrain. My eye
Caught in those flags a gravestone's fragment
 Set by a careful century. The washed inscription
Still keen, showed only by a fragile stem
 A stave, a broken circlet, as
(Unintelligibly clear, craft in the sharp decrepitude)
 A pothook grooved its firm memorial.

Within, wet from the failing roof,
　　Walls greened. Each hearth re-fitted
For a suburban whim, each room
　　Denied what it was, diminished thus
To a barbarous mean, had comforted (but for a time)
　　Its latest tenant. Angered, I turned to my path
Through the inhuman light, light that a fish might swim
　　Stained by the greyness of the smoking fields.

Five centuries. And we? What we had not
　　Made ugly, we had laid waste—
Left (I should say) the office to nature
　　Whose blind battery, best fitted to perform it
Outdoes us, completes by persistence
　　All that our negligence fails in. Saddened,
Yet angered beyond sadness, where the road
　　Doubled upon itself I halted, for a moment
Facing the empty house and its laden barns.

*

From ANTECEDENTS

VI

SOMETHING: A DIRECTION

Out of the shut cell of that solitude there is
　　One egress, past point of interrogation.
Sun is, because it is not you; you are
　　Since you are self, and self delimited
Regarding sun. It downs? I claim? Cannot
　　Beyond such speech as this, gather conviction?
Judge, as you will, not what I say
　　But what is, being said. It downs
Recovered, coverless, in a shriven light

And you, returning, may to a shriven self
As from the scene, your self withdraws. You are downing
    Back from that autumn music of the light, which
Split by your need, to know the textures of your pain,
    Refuses them in your acceptance. You accept
An evening, washed of its over-tones
    By strict seclusion, yet are not secluded
Withheld at your proper bounds. From there
    Your returns may enter, welcome strangers
Into a civil country (you were not the first
    To see it), but a country, natural and profuse
Unbroken by past incursions, as the theme
    Strung over stave, is rediscovered
After dismemberment in the canon, and over stave
    Can still proceed, unwound, unwinding
To its established presence, its territory
    Staked and sunk; and the phrase descends
As a phase concluded. Released
    From knowing to acknowledgement, from prison
To powers, you are new-found
    Neighboured, having earned relation
With all that is other. Still you must wait,
    For evening's ashen, like the slow fire
Withdrawn through the whitened log
    Glinting through grainmarks where the wood splits:
Let be its being: the scene extends
    Not hope, but the urgency that hopes for means.

*

ENTERING AUTUMN

ENTERING autumn, there ensues
    (Its beauty is in brevity)
A season of crystalline repose,
Still day with lucent dusk . . .

Steady incursion of the blade
Lets space into the crop:
Emptiness over all, save where
Cobweb on idle furrow
Stretches its gleam of subtle hair.

Birdless, the vacant atmosphere;
But the first tempests lie
Folded, as liquid, mild
Warm-blue keeps winter from the resting field.

*

WINTER-PIECE

You wake, all windows blind—embattled sprays
grained on the medieval glass.
Gates snap like gunshot
as you handle them. Five-barred fragility
sets flying fifteen rooks who go together
silently ravenous above this winter-piece
that will not feed them. They alight
beyond, scavenging, missing everything
but the bladed atmosphere, the white resistance.
Ruts with iron flanges track
through a hard decay
where you discern once more
oak-leaf by hawthorn, for the frost
rewhets their edges. In a perfect web
blanched along each spoke
and circle of its woven wheel,
the spider hangs, grasp unbroken
and death-masked in cold. Returning
you see the house glint-out behind
its holed and ragged glaze,
frost-fronds all streaming.

*

WHAT IT WAS LIKE

It was like the approach of flame
treading the tinder, a fleet
cascade of it taking tree-toll,
halting below the hill and then
covering the corn-field's dryness
in an effortless crescendo. One heard
in the pause of the receding silence
the whole house grow
tense through its ties, the beams
brace beneath pan-tiles
for the coming burst. It came
and went. The blinded pane
emerged from the rainsheet
to an after-water world,
its green confusion brought
closer greener. The baptism
of the shining house was done
and it was like the calm
a church aisle harbours
tasting of incense, space and stone.

*

HOW IT HAPPENED

It happened like this: I heard
from the farm beyond, a grounded
churn go down. The sound
chimed for the wedding of the mind
with what one could not see,
the further fields, the seamless
spread of space, and then,
all bestial ease, the cows
foregathered by the milking place
in a placid stupor. There are two
ways to marry with a land—

first, this bland and blind
submergence of the self, an act
of kind and questionless. The other
is the thing I mean, a whole
event, a happening, the sound
that brings all space in
for its bound, when self is clear
as what we keenest see and hear :
no absolute of eye can tell
the utmost, but the glance
goes shafted from us like a well.

*

UP AT LA SERRA

THE shadow
        ran before it lengthening
                and a wave went over.

Distance
        did not obscure
                the machine of nature :

you could watch it
        squander and recompose itself
                all day, the shadow-run

the sway of the necessity down there
        at the cliff-base
                crushing white from blue.

Come in
        by the arch
                under the campanile parrocchiale

and the exasperation of the water
        followed you
                its *Soldi, soldi*

unpicking the hill-top peace
        insistently.
                He knew, at twenty

all the deprivations such a place
                    stored for the man
                              who had no more to offer
than a sheaf of verse
                    in the style of Quasimodo.
                              Came the moment,
he would tell it
          in a poem
                    without rancour, a lucid
testament above his name
                    Paolo
                              Bertolani
—*Ciao, Paolo!*
          —*Giorgino*
                    Ciao!
He would put them
          all in it—
                    Giorgino going
over the hill
          to look for labour;
                    the grinder
of knives and scissors
          waiting to come up, until
                    someone would hoist his wheel
on to a back, already
          hooped to take it,
                    so you thought
the weight must crack
          the curvature. And then :
                    Beppino and Beppino
friends
          who had in common
                    nothing except their names and friendship;
and the sister of the one
          who played the accordion
                    and under all
the *Soldi, soldi,*
          sacra conversazione

88

                    del mare—
della madre.
                    Sometimes
                            the men had an air of stupefaction :
La Madre:
                    it was the women there
                            won in a truceless enmity.
At home
            a sepia-green
                    Madonna di Foligno
shared the wall
            with the October calendar—
                    Lenin looked out of it,
Mao
            blessing the tractors
                    and you told
the visitors :
            We are not communists
                    although we call ourselves communists
we are what you English
            would call . . . socialists.
                            He believed
that God was a hypothesis,
            that the party would bring in
                    a synthesis, that he
would edit the local paper for them,
            or perhaps
                    go northward to Milan;
or would he grow
            as the others had—son
                    to the putana-madonna
in the curse,
            chafed by the maternal knot and by
                    the dream of faithlessness,
uncalloused hands,
            lace, white
                    at the windows of the sailors' brothels
in the port five miles away?

                    Soldi
                              soldi—
some
          worked at the naval yards
                    and some, like him
were left between
          the time the olives turned
                    from green to black
and the harvest of the grapes,
          idle
                    except for hacking wood.
Those
          with an acre of good land
                    had vines, had wine
and self-respect. Some
          carried down crickets
                    to the garden of the mad Englishwoman
who could
          not
                    tolerate
crickets, and they received
          soldi, soldi
                    for recapturing them . . .
The construction
          continued as heretofore
                    on the villa of the Milanese dentist
as the evening
          came in with news:
                    —We have won
the election.
                    —At the café
                              the red flag is up.
He turned back
          quickly beneath the tower.
                              Giorgino
who wanted to be a waiter
          wanted to be a commissar
                    piling *sassi*

into the dentist's wall.
                    Even the harlot's mother
                                    who had not dared
come forth because her daughter
                    had erred in giving birth,
                                    appeared by the *Trattoria della Pace.*

She did not enter
                    the masculine precinct,
                                    listening there, her shadow
lengthened-out behind her
                    black as the uniform of age
                                    she wore
on back and head.
                    This was the Day
                                    which began all reckonings
she heard them say
                    with a woman's ears;
                                    she liked
the music from the wireless.
                    The padre
                                    pulled
at his unheeded angelus
                    and the Day went down behind
                                    the town in the bay below
where—come the season—
                    they would be preparing
                                    with striped umbrellas,
for the *stranieri* and *milanesi*—
                    treason so readily compounded
                                    by the promiscuous stir
on the iridescent sliding water.
                    He had sought
                                    the clear air of the cliff.
—*Salve, Giorgino*
                    —*Salve*
                                    Paolo, have you
heard
                    that we have won the election?

—I am writing
a poem about it;
         it will begin
               here, with the cliff and with the sea
following its morning shadow in.

*

CANAL

    SWANS. I watch them
    come unsteadying
    the dusty, green
    and curving arm
    of water. Sinuously
    both the live
    bird and the bird
    the water bends
    into a white and wandering
    reflection of itself,
    go by in grace
    a world of objects.
    Symmetrically punched
    now empty rivet-
    holes betray
    a sleeper fence:
    below its raggedness
    the waters darken
    and above it rear
    the saw-toothed houses
    which the swinging
    of the waters makes
    scarcely less regular
    in repetition. Swans
    are backed by these, as
    these are by
    a sky of silhouettes,

all black and almost
all, indefinite.
A whitish smoke
in drifting diagonals
accents, divides
the predominance of street-
and chimney-lines,
where all is either
mathematically supine
or vertical, except
the pyramids of slag.
And, there, unseen
among such angularities—
a church, a black
freestanding witness
that a space of graves
invisibly is also
there. Only
its clock identifies
the tower between
the accompaniment of stacks
where everything
repeats itself—
the slag, the streets
and water that repeats
them all again
and spreads them rippling
out beneath
the eye of the discriminating
swans that seek
for something else
and the blank brink
concludes them without conclusion.

*

HEAD HEWN WITH AN AXE

THE whittled crystal: fissured
For the invasion of shadows.

The stone book, its
Hacked leaves
Frozen in granite.

The meteorite, anatomized
By the geometer. And to what end?
To the enrichment of the alignment:
Sun against shade against sun:
That daily food, which
Were it not for such importunities
Would go untasted:

The suave block, desecrated
In six strokes. The light
Is staunching its wounds.

*

THE PICTURE OF J.T.
IN A PROSPECT OF STONE

WHAT should one
         wish a child
                  and that, one's own
emerging
         from between
                  the stone lips
of a sheep-stile

that divides
village graves
and village green?
—Wish her
the constancy of stone.
—But stone
is hard.
—Say, rather
it resists
the slow corrosives
and the flight
of time
and yet it takes
the play, the fluency
from light.
—How would you know
the gift you'd give
was the gift
she'd wish to have?
—Gift is giving,
gift is meaning:
first
I'd give
then let her
live with it
to prove
its quality the better and
thus learn
to love
what (to begin with)
she might spurn.
—You'd
moralize a gift?
—I'd have her
understand
the gift I gave her.
—And so she shall
but let her play

her innocence away
                    emerging
                              as she does
          between
                    her doom (unknown),
                              her unmown green.

                              *

LAMENT OF THE VIRTUES AND VERSES ON ACCOUNT OF THE DEATH OF DON GUIDO

IT was pneumonia
finally carried away
Don Guido, and so the bells
(*din-dan*) toll for him the whole day.

Died Don Guido
gentleman; when younger
great at gallantry and roistering,
a minor talent in the bullring—
older, his prayers grew longer.

This Sevillan gentleman
kept (so they say)
a seraglio, was apt
at managing a horse
and a master
at cooling manzanilla.

When his riches dwindled
it was his obsession
to think that he ought to think
of settling in quiet possession.

And he settled
in a very Spanish way
which was—to marry
a maiden of large fortune
and to repaint his blazons,
to refer to the traditions of
'this house of ours',
setting a measure
to scandals and amours
and damping down the expenditure on pleasure.

He became, great pagan
that he was,
brother in a fraternity;
on Holy Thursday could be seen
disguised
(the immense candle in his hand)
in the long robe of a Nazarene.

Today
you may hear the bell
say that the good Don Guido
with solemn face
tomorrow must go
the slow road to the burial place.
For ever and for always
gone, good Don Guido . . .
'What have you left?' some will say—
I ask, 'What have you taken
to the world in which you are today?'

Your love for braid
and for silks and gold
and the blood of bulls and the fume that rolled
from off the altars.

To good Don Guido and his equipage
bon voyage!

The here
and the there,
cavalier,
show in your withered face,
confess the infinite :
the nothingness.

On the thin cheeks
yellow
and the eyelids, wax,
and the delicate skull
on the bed's pillow!

Oh end of an aristocracy!
The beard on breast
lies limp and hoary,
in the rough serge
of a monk he's dressed;
crossed, the hands that cannot stir
and the Andalusian gentleman
on his best behaviour.

*

UTE MOUNTAIN

'WHEN I am gone'
the old chief said
'if you need me, call me,'
and down he lay, became stone.

They were giants then
(as you may see),
and we
are not the shadows of such men.

The long splayed Indian hair
spread ravelling out
behind the rocky head
in groins, ravines;

petered across the desert plain
through Colorado,
transmitting force
in a single undulant unbroken line

from toe to hair-tip : there
profiled, inclined away from one
are features, foreshortened, and the high
blade of the cheekbone.

Reading it so, the eye
can take the entire great
straddle of mountain-mass,
passing down elbows, knees, and feet.

'If you need me, call me.'
His singularity dominates the plain
as we call to our aid his image :
thus men make a mountain.

*

AT BARSTOW

NERVY with neons, the main drag
was all there was. A placeless place.
A faint flavour of Mexico in the tacos
tasting of gasoline. Trucks refuelled
before taking off through space. Someone lived
in the houses with their houseyards wired
like tiny Belsens. The Götterdämmerung
would be like this. No funeral pyres, no choirs

of lost trombones. An Untergang
without a clang, without
a glimmer of gone glory
however dimmed. At the motel desk
was a photograph of Roy Rogers
signed. It was here
he made a stay. He did not
ride away on Trigger
through the high night, the tilted
Pleiades overhead, the polestar low, no
going off until
the eyes of beer-cans
had ceased to glint at him
and the desert darknesses
had quenched the neons. He was spent.
He was content. Down he lay.
The passing trucks patrolled his sleep,
the shifted gears contrived
a muffled fugue against the fading of his day
and his dustless, undishonoured stetson rode
beside the bed,
glowed in the pulsating, never-final twilight
there, at that execrable conjunction
of gasoline and desert air.

*

MR. BRODSKY

I HAD heard
before, of an
American who would have preferred
to be an Indian;
but not
until Mr. Brodsky, of one

whose professed and long
pondered-on passion
was to become a Scot,
who even sent for haggis and oatcakes
across continent.
Having read him
in Cambridge English
a verse or two
from MacDiarmid,
I was invited
to repeat the reading
before a Burns Night Gathering
where the Balmoral Pipers
of Albuquerque would
play in the haggis
out of its New York tin.
Of course, I said
No. No, I could *not* go
and then
half-regretted I had not been.
But to console
and cure the wish, came
Mr. Brodsky, bringing
his pipes and played
until the immense, distended
bladder of leather seemed
it could barely contain its water—
tears (idle
tears) for the bridal of Annie Laurie
and Morton J. Brodsky.
A bagpipe in a dwelling is
a resonant instrument
and there he stood
lost in the gorse
the heather or whatever
six thousand
miles and more
from the infection's source,

in our neo-New Mexican parlour
where I had heard
before of an
American who would have preferred
to be merely an Indian.

*

THE CAVERN

OBLITERATE
mythology as you unwind
this mountain-interior
into the negative-dark mind,
as there
the gypsum's snow
the limestone stair
and boneyard landscape grow
into the identity of flesh.

Pulse of the water-drop,
veils and scales, fins
and flakes of the forming
leprous rock,
how should these
inhuman, turn
human with such chill affinities.

Hard to the hand,
these mosses not of moss,
but nostrils, pits
of eyes, faces
in flight and prints
of feet where no feet ever were,
elude the mind's
hollow that would contain
this canyon within a mountain.

Not far
enough from the familiar,
press
in under a deeper dark until
the curtained sex
the arch the streaming buttress
have become
the self's unnameable and shaping home.